Making
Animal
Pulltoys

Making Animal Pulltoys

Patterns and Instructions for 14 Easy Projects

by

ED SIBBETT, JR.

Dover Publications, Inc., New York

Published in Canada by General Publishing Company, Ltd., 30 Lesmill Road, Don Mills, Toronto, Ontario.
Published in the United Kingdom by Constable and Company, Ltd., 10 Orange Street, London WC2H 7EG.

Making Animal Pulltoys: Patterns and Instructions for 14 Easy Projects is a new work, first published by Dover Publications, Inc., in 1990.

Manufactured in the United States of America
Dover Publications, Inc., 31 East 2nd Street, Mineola, N.Y. 11501

Library of Congress Cataloging-in-Publication Data

Sibbett, Ed.
    Making animal pulltoys : patterns and instructions for 14 easy projects / by Ed Sibbett, Jr.
        p.   cm.
    ISBN 0-486-26249-9
    1. Wooden toy making.   2. Animals in art.   I. Title.
TT174.5.W6S53   1990
745.592—dc20   89-29971
                                                                        CIP

CONTENTS

INSTRUCTIONS

Nothing, except perhaps their own living playmates and pets, offers such great companionship to young children as their baby-animal counterparts in the form of painted wooden pulltoys. With the patterns and instructions in this book, even if you are a woodworker with limited experience, you can easily make these fourteen lively, sturdy toys that will long be treasured by the children you treasure most. You will need only the following easily obtainable tools and materials.

Tools and Materials

Powered, table-mounted scroll saw or jigsaw
Drill with ¼″ and ⁵⁄₁₆″ bits
Carbon paper
Tracing paper
Pencil
Wood in various lengths and widths (good-quality pine shelving is usually satisfactory), ³⁄₃₂″, ½″, ⅝″, and ¾″ thick (you may have to purchase larger nominal sizes to obtain these actual sizes—check with your lumber dealer)
Wood dowels, ¼″ in diameter
Medium and fine grades of sandpaper
Nontoxic glue
Nontoxic paints
Screweye

Making the Base

The wheeled base is the same for all the toys. It is made from the patterns on Plate 1. The ¼″-diameter dowels are of course purchased already cut in cylindrical form; the patterns are meant only as a guide to length (3⁵⁄₁₆″). The four wheels should be cut from a suitable length of board 1½″–2″ wide and ½″ thick. If you can obtain a 1½″-diameter cylinder of wood and simply slice off four wheels, so much the better. Perhaps the best way of all for producing evenly rounded wheels is by using a hole saw and mandrel. Whichever method you use, remember that the wheels must all be the same and the hole must be drilled straight through the exact center. The wheels should be smooth and evenly rounded as well, or the toy simply will not roll properly.

The base itself is 8″ long × 2¼″ wide × ⅝–¾″ thick. Drill ¼″ holes in the wheels and ⁵⁄₁₆″ holes through the base as marked on the patterns. Paint the base and wheels. Let the paint dry. Insert the dowels in the base and glue the wheels on. When the glue has dried, sand and paint the ends of the dowels. An attachment for pulling the toy is easily made by inserting a screweye at one end of the base. Now you are ready to complete an individual toy.

Cutting and Finishing the Toy

Examine the patterns for the project of your choice and obtain wood of suitable dimensions for each piece. Arms, legs, and wings should be cut from wood ³⁄₃₂″ thick. Some tails may be about ½″ thick, others, like the raccoon's tail, are better at the full ¾″ thickness. The beaver's tail is made of a suitable length of ¾″ × ¾″ board. The bodies should be ¾″ thick. Objects held between arms and legs (like the rabbit's carrot and dog's bone) must be exactly the same thickness as the bodies. For certain pieces (the body of the raccoon, for example), it may be difficult to obtain wood of suitable dimensions. These pieces may be cut out in separate sections—most often body and tail separately—and then glued together.

Now it is necessary to transfer the patterns onto the wood. There are many methods for accomplishing this. One simple way is to use tracing paper and carbon paper. First place a sheet of tracing paper over the patterns for the toy you wish to make. Using an ordinary lead pencil, trace the outlines of the parts, as well as all lines within these outlines. The solid lines separate the different areas where paint is to be applied, and dashed lines show where other parts are to be glued on. The small illustration on the pattern plate(s) for each project shows how the finished pulltoy will look. Use this illustration also to identify each part so you can know what thickness of wood to use for it.

Next, tack the tracing paper in place over the wood and insert a sheet of carbon paper. Go over the outlines carefully with a stylus or pencil. Do not remove the tracing paper until you are sure that all lines have been transferred onto the wood. (Note: the grain of the wood should always run along the *longest* dimension of the piece.) Once the wood pieces have been cut out, you can transfer the painting lines to the other side as follows.

Flop the tracing paper (i.e., flip it over to show a mirror image) and align it carefully. Lightly tack or tape down the tracing paper. Insert carbon paper and retrace the solid and dashed lines. If more convenient, use a small piece of carbon paper and move it around as needed.

Once again, be sure that all lines appear properly before you completely remove the tracing paper.

When you have traced the patterns onto the wood, cut carefully around the outside of the outlines. A powered, table-mounted scroll saw or jigsaw is usually necessary for this, but experienced woodworkers may be able to cut out the shapes with a hand-held coping saw. Smooth all rough surfaces with sandpaper.

Next, glue the pieces together. When the glue has dried, paint all but the very bottom, where the animal is to be glued onto the base. (Always use nontoxic paints on toys that are to be handled by young children.) After the paint has dried, the animal can be glued to its base. You may need to sand away some of the paint on the top of the base (or, alternatively, wait until the animal is glued in place before painting the top of the base). This completes the pulltoy.

Making
Animal
Pulltoys

Plate 1

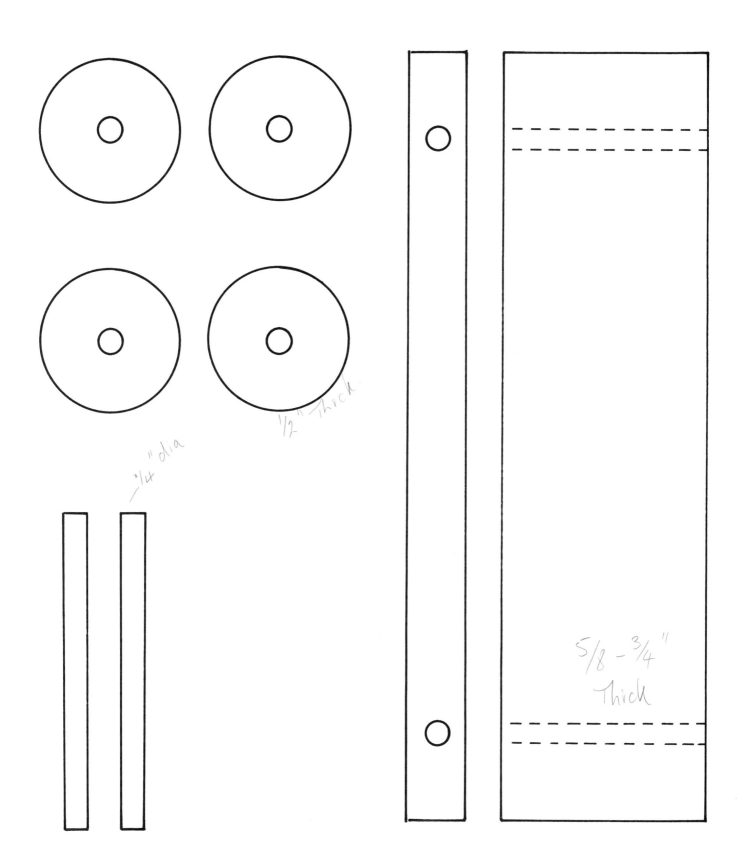

BASE

Plate 2

BEAR

Plate 3

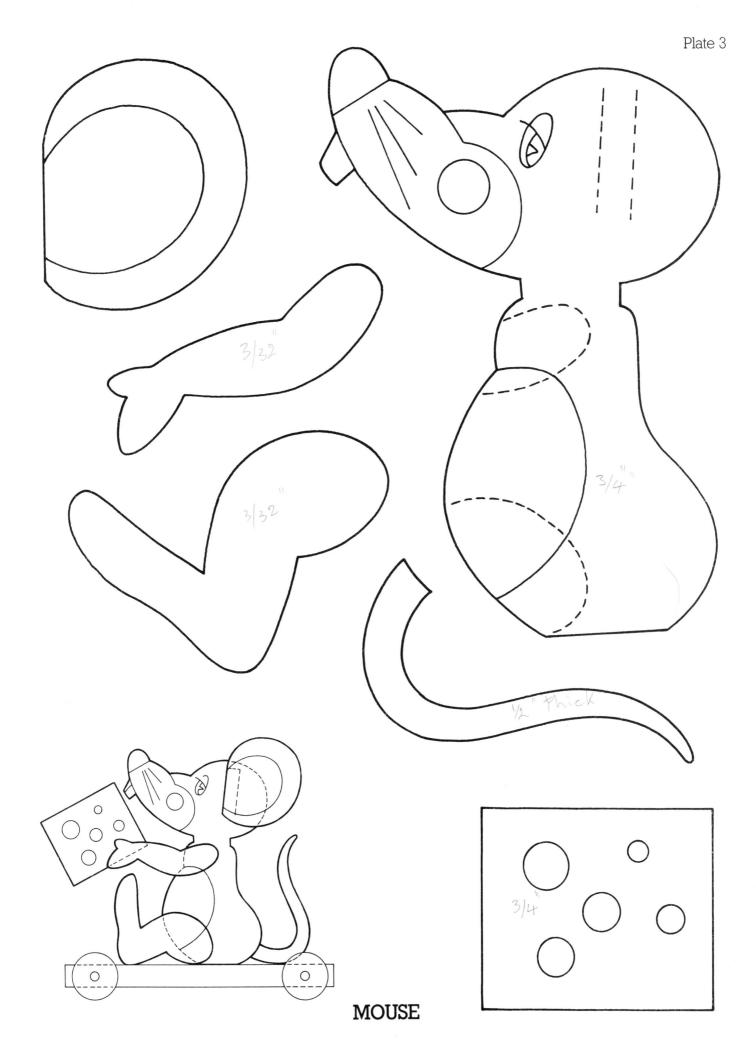

3/32"

3/32"

3/4"

3/4"

½" thick

MOUSE

Plate 4

DUCK

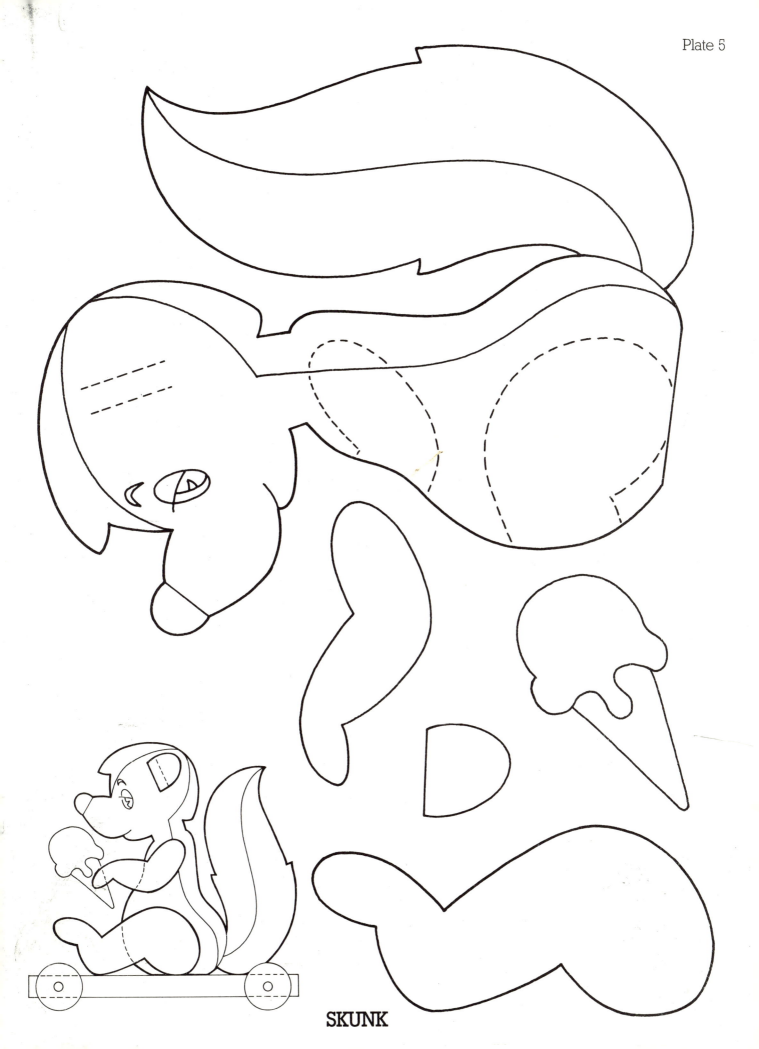

Plate 5

SKUNK

Plate 6

MONKEY

Plate 7

PIG

Plate 8

GIRAFFE

Plate 9

FROG

Plate 10

SQUIRREL

Plate 11

CAT

Plate 12

BEAVER (I)

Plate 13

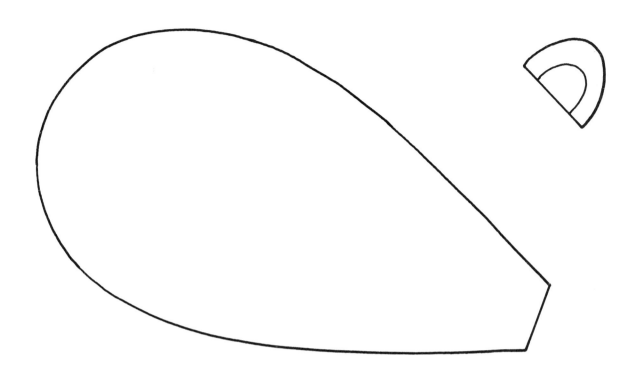

BEAVER (II)

Plate 14

DOG

Plate 15

RABBIT

Plate 16

RACCOON